THIS PLANNER BELONGS TO:

_____

CONTACTS

NAME	ADDRESS	NUMBERS

2021

JANUARY

SUN	MON	TUE	WED	THU	FRI	SAT
					1	2
3	4	5	6	7	8	9
10	11	12	13	14	15	16
17	18	19	20	21	22	23
24	25	26	27	28	29	30
31						

FEBRUARY

SUN	MON	TUE	WED	THU	FRI	SAT
	1	2	3	4	5	6
7	8	9	10	11	12	13
14	15	16	17	18	19	20
21	22	23	24	25	26	27
28						

MARCH

SUN	MON	TUE	WED	THU	FRI	SAT
	1	2	3	4	5	6
7	8	9	10	11	12	13
14	15	16	17	18	19	20
21	22	23	24	25	26	27
28	29	30	31			

APRIL

SUN	MON	TUE	WED	THU	FRI	SAT
				1	2	3
4	5	6	7	8	9	10
11	12	13	14	15	16	17
18	19	20	21	22	23	24
25	26	27	28	29	30	

MAY

SUN	MON	TUE	WED	THU	FRI	SAT
						1
2	3	4	5	6	7	8
9	10	11	12	13	14	15
16	17	18	19	20	21	22
23	24	25	26	27	28	29
30	31					

JUNE

SUN	MON	TUE	WED	THU	FRI	SAT
		1	2	3	4	5
6	7	8	9	10	11	12
13	14	15	16	17	18	19
20	21	22	23	24	25	26
27	28	29	30			

JULY

SUN	MON	TUE	WED	THU	FRI	SAT
				1	2	3
4	5	6	7	8	9	10
11	12	13	14	15	16	17
18	19	20	21	22	23	24
25	26	27	28	29	30	31

AUGUST

SUN	MON	TUE	WED	THU	FRI	SAT
1	2	3	4	5	6	7
8	9	10	11	12	13	14
15	16	17	18	19	20	21
22	23	24	25	26	27	28
29	30	31				

SEPTEMBER

SUN	MON	TUE	WED	THU	FRI	SAT
			1	2	3	4
5	6	7	8	9	10	11
12	13	14	15	16	17	18
19	20	21	22	23	24	25
26	27	28	29	30		

OCTOBER

SUN	MON	TUE	WED	THU	FRI	SAT
					1	2
3	4	5	6	7	8	9
10	11	12	13	14	15	16
17	18	19	20	21	22	23
24	25	26	27	28	29	30
31						

NOVEMBER

SUN	MON	TUE	WED	THU	FRI	SAT
	1	2	3	4	5	6
7	8	9	10	11	12	13
14	15	16	17	18	19	20
21	22	23	24	25	26	27
28	29	30				

DECEMBER

SUN	MON	TUE	WED	THU	FRI	SAT
			1	2	3	4
5	6	7	8	9	10	11
12	13	14	15	16	17	18
19	20	21	22	23	24	25
26	27	28	29	30	31	

IMPORTANT DATES

January 2021

SUNDAY	MONDAY	TUESDAY	WEDNESDAY
3	4	5	6
10	11	12	13
17	18 Martin Luther King, Jr. Day	19	20
24	25	26	27
31			

THURSDAY	FRIDAY	SATURDAY	NOTES
	1 New Year's Day	**2**	
7	**8**	**9**	
14	**15**	**16**	
21	**22**	**23**	
28	**29**	**30**	

December 2020

28 MONDAY

☐
☐
☐
☐
☐
☐
☐
☐
☐
☐
☐

29 TUESDAY

☐
☐
☐
☐
☐
☐
☐
☐
☐
☐
☐

30 WEDNESDAY

☐
☐
☐
☐
☐
☐
☐
☐
☐
☐
☐

December 2020

31 THURSDAY

New Year's Eve

☐
☐
☐
☐
☐
☐
☐
☐
☐
☐
☐

1 FRIDAY

New Year's Day

☐
☐
☐
☐
☐
☐
☐
☐
☐
☐
☐

2 SATURDAY

3 SUNDAY

January 2021

4 MONDAY

_____
_____
_____
_____
_____
_____
_____
_____
_____
_____

☐
☐
☐
☐
☐
☐
☐
☐
☐
☐
☐

5 TUESDAY

_____
_____
_____
_____
_____
_____
_____
_____
_____
_____

☐
☐
☐
☐
☐
☐
☐
☐
☐
☐
☐

6 WEDNESDAY

_____
_____
_____
_____
_____
_____
_____
_____
_____
_____

☐
☐
☐
☐
☐
☐
☐
☐
☐
☐
☐

7 THURSDAY

☐
☐
☐
☐
☐
☐
☐
☐
☐
☐
☐

8 FRIDAY

☐
☐
☐
☐
☐
☐
☐
☐
☐
☐
☐

9 SATURDAY

10 SUNDAY

January 2021

11 MONDAY

☐
☐
☐
☐
☐
☐
☐
☐
☐
☐
☐

12 TUESDAY

☐
☐
☐
☐
☐
☐
☐
☐
☐
☐
☐

13 WEDNESDAY

☐
☐
☐
☐
☐
☐
☐
☐
☐
☐
☐

14 THURSDAY

☐
☐
☐
☐
☐
☐
☐
☐
☐
☐
☐

15 FRIDAY

☐
☐
☐
☐
☐
☐
☐
☐
☐
☐
☐

16 SATURDAY

17 SUNDAY

January 2021

18 **MONDAY**

Martin Luther King, Jr. Day

☐
☐
☐
☐
☐
☐
☐
☐
☐
☐
☐

19 **TUESDAY**

☐
☐
☐
☐
☐
☐
☐
☐
☐
☐
☐

20 **WEDNESDAY**

☐
☐
☐
☐
☐
☐
☐
☐
☐
☐
☐

21 THURSDAY

☐
☐
☐
☐
☐
☐
☐
☐
☐
☐
☐

22 FRIDAY

☐
☐
☐
☐
☐
☐
☐
☐
☐
☐
☐

23 SATURDAY

24 SUNDAY

January 2021

25 MONDAY

_____
_____
_____
_____
_____
_____
_____
_____
_____
_____
_____

- ☐
- ☐
- ☐
- ☐
- ☐
- ☐
- ☐
- ☐
- ☐
- ☐
- ☐

26 TUESDAY

_____
_____
_____
_____
_____
_____
_____
_____
_____
_____
_____

- ☐
- ☐
- ☐
- ☐
- ☐
- ☐
- ☐
- ☐
- ☐
- ☐
- ☐

27 WEDNESDAY

_____
_____
_____
_____
_____
_____
_____
_____
_____
_____

- ☐
- ☐
- ☐
- ☐
- ☐
- ☐
- ☐
- ☐
- ☐
- ☐
- ☐

January 2021

28 THURSDAY

☐
☐
☐
☐
☐
☐
☐
☐
☐
☐
☐

29 FRIDAY

☐
☐
☐
☐
☐
☐
☐
☐
☐
☐
☐

30 SATURDAY

31 SUNDAY

February 2021

SUNDAY	MONDAY	TUESDAY	WEDNESDAY
	1	2	3
7	8	9	10
14 Valentine's Day	15 Presidents' Day	16	17 Ash Wednesday
21	22	23	24
28			

THURSDAY	FRIDAY	SATURDAY	NOTES
4	5	6	
11	12	13	
18	19	20	
25	26	27	

February 2021

1 **MONDAY**

☐
☐
☐
☐
☐
☐
☐
☐
☐
☐
☐

2 **TUESDAY**

☐
☐
☐
☐
☐
☐
☐
☐
☐
☐
☐

3 **WEDNESDAY**

☐
☐
☐
☐
☐
☐
☐
☐
☐
☐
☐

February 2021

4 THURSDAY

☐
☐
☐
☐
☐
☐
☐
☐
☐
☐
☐

5 FRIDAY

☐
☐
☐
☐
☐
☐
☐
☐
☐
☐
☐

6 SATURDAY

7 SUNDAY

February 2021

8 MONDAY

☐
☐
☐
☐
☐
☐
☐
☐
☐
☐

9 TUESDAY

☐
☐
☐
☐
☐
☐
☐
☐
☐
☐

10 WEDNESDAY

☐
☐
☐
☐
☐
☐
☐
☐
☐
☐
☐

February 2021

11 THURSDAY

- ☐
- ☐
- ☐
- ☐
- ☐
- ☐
- ☐
- ☐
- ☐
- ☐
- ☐

12 FRIDAY

- ☐
- ☐
- ☐
- ☐
- ☐
- ☐
- ☐
- ☐
- ☐
- ☐
- ☐

13 SATURDAY

14 SUNDAY

Valentine's Day

February 2021

15 MONDAY
Presidents' Day

- [ ]
- [ ]
- [ ]
- [ ]
- [ ]
- [ ]
- [ ]
- [ ]
- [ ]
- [ ]
- [ ]

16 TUESDAY

- [ ]
- [ ]
- [ ]
- [ ]
- [ ]
- [ ]
- [ ]
- [ ]
- [ ]
- [ ]
- [ ]

17 WEDNESDAY
Ash Wednesday

- [ ]
- [ ]
- [ ]
- [ ]
- [ ]
- [ ]
- [ ]
- [ ]
- [ ]
- [ ]
- [ ]
- [ ]

February 2021

18 THURSDAY

- [ ]
- [ ]
- [ ]
- [ ]
- [ ]
- [ ]
- [ ]
- [ ]
- [ ]
- [ ]
- [ ]

19 FRIDAY

- [ ]
- [ ]
- [ ]
- [ ]
- [ ]
- [ ]
- [ ]
- [ ]
- [ ]
- [ ]
- [ ]

20 SATURDAY

21 SUNDAY

February 2021

22 MONDAY

☐
☐
☐
☐
☐
☐
☐
☐
☐
☐
☐

23 TUESDAY

☐
☐
☐
☐
☐
☐
☐
☐
☐
☐
☐

24 WEDNESDAY

☐
☐
☐
☐
☐
☐
☐
☐
☐
☐
☐

February 2021

25 THURSDAY

☐
☐
☐
☐
☐
☐
☐
☐
☐
☐
☐

26 FRIDAY

☐
☐
☐
☐
☐
☐
☐
☐
☐
☐
☐
☐

27 SATURDAY

28 SUNDAY

March 2021

SUNDAY	MONDAY	TUESDAY	WEDNESDAY
	1	2	3
7	8	9	10
14 Daylight Saving Time Begins	15	16	17 St. Patrick's Day
21	22	23	24
28 Palm Sunday	29	30	31

THURSDAY	FRIDAY	SATURDAY	NOTES
4	**5**	**6**	
11	**12**	**13**	
18	**19**	**20** First Day of Spring	
25	**26**	**27** Passover, Begins at Sunset	

March 2021

1 **MONDAY**

_____
_____
_____
_____
_____
_____
_____
_____
_____

☐
☐
☐
☐
☐
☐
☐
☐
☐
☐
☐

2 **TUESDAY**

_____
_____
_____
_____
_____
_____
_____
_____
_____

☐
☐
☐
☐
☐
☐
☐
☐
☐
☐
☐

3 **WEDNESDAY**

_____
_____
_____
_____
_____
_____
_____
_____
_____

☐
☐
☐
☐
☐
☐
☐
☐
☐
☐
☐

March 2021

4 THURSDAY

☐
☐
☐
☐
☐
☐
☐
☐
☐
☐
☐

5 FRIDAY

☐
☐
☐
☐
☐
☐
☐
☐
☐
☐
☐

6 SATURDAY

7 SUNDAY

March 2021

8 **MONDAY**

☐
☐
☐
☐
☐
☐
☐
☐
☐
☐
☐

9 **TUESDAY**

☐
☐
☐
☐
☐
☐
☐
☐
☐
☐
☐

10 **WEDNESDAY**

☐
☐
☐
☐
☐
☐
☐
☐
☐
☐
☐

11 **THURSDAY**

☐
☐
☐
☐
☐
☐
☐
☐
☐
☐
☐

12 **FRIDAY**

☐
☐
☐
☐
☐
☐
☐
☐
☐
☐
☐

13 **SATURDAY**

14 **SUNDAY**

Daylight Saving Time Begins

March 2021

15 MONDAY

☐
☐
☐
☐
☐
☐
☐
☐
☐
☐
☐

16 TUESDAY

☐
☐
☐
☐
☐
☐
☐
☐
☐
☐
☐

17 WEDNESDAY

St. Patrick's Day

☐
☐
☐
☐
☐
☐
☐
☐
☐
☐
☐

March 2021

18 THURSDAY

- [ ]
- [ ]
- [ ]
- [ ]
- [ ]
- [ ]
- [ ]
- [ ]
- [ ]
- [ ]
- [ ]

19 FRIDAY

- [ ]
- [ ]
- [ ]
- [ ]
- [ ]
- [ ]
- [ ]
- [ ]
- [ ]
- [ ]
- [ ]

20 SATURDAY

First Day of Spring

21 SUNDAY

March 2021

22 MONDAY

☐
☐
☐
☐
☐
☐
☐
☐
☐
☐
☐

23 TUESDAY

☐
☐
☐
☐
☐
☐
☐
☐
☐
☐
☐

24 WEDNESDAY

☐
☐
☐
☐
☐
☐
☐
☐
☐
☐
☐

March 2021

25 THURSDAY

☐
☐
☐
☐
☐
☐
☐
☐
☐
☐
☐

26 FRIDAY

☐
☐
☐
☐
☐
☐
☐
☐
☐
☐
☐

27 SATURDAY

Passover, Begins at Sunset

28 SUNDAY

Palm Sunday

April 2021

SUNDAY	MONDAY	TUESDAY	WEDNESDAY
4 Easter	5	6	7
11	12	13	14
18	19	20	21
25	26	27	28

THURSDAY	FRIDAY	SATURDAY	NOTES
1	**2** Good Friday	**3**	
8	**9**	**10**	
15	**16**	**17**	
22 Earth Day	**23**	**24**	
29	**30**		

March 2021

29 MONDAY

_____
_____
_____
_____
_____
_____
_____
_____
_____
_____

☐
☐
☐
☐
☐
☐
☐
☐
☐
☐
☐

30 TUESDAY

_____
_____
_____
_____
_____
_____
_____
_____
_____
_____

☐
☐
☐
☐
☐
☐
☐
☐
☐
☐
☐

31 WEDNESDAY

_____
_____
_____
_____
_____
_____
_____
_____
_____
_____

☐
☐
☐
☐
☐
☐
☐
☐
☐
☐
☐

April 2021

1 THURSDAY

☐
☐
☐
☐
☐
☐
☐
☐
☐
☐
☐

2 FRIDAY

Good Friday

☐
☐
☐
☐
☐
☐
☐
☐
☐
☐
☐

3 SATURDAY

4 SUNDAY

Easter

April 2021

5 MONDAY

☐
☐
☐
☐
☐
☐
☐
☐
☐
☐
☐

6 TUESDAY

☐
☐
☐
☐
☐
☐
☐
☐
☐
☐

7 WEDNESDAY

☐
☐
☐
☐
☐
☐
☐
☐
☐
☐
☐

April 2021

8 THURSDAY

☐
☐
☐
☐
☐
☐
☐
☐
☐
☐
☐

9 FRIDAY

☐
☐
☐
☐
☐
☐
☐
☐
☐
☐
☐

10 SATURDAY

11 SUNDAY

April 2021

12 MONDAY

_____ ☐ _____
_____ ☐ _____
_____ ☐ _____
_____ ☐ _____
_____ ☐ _____
_____ ☐ _____
_____ ☐ _____
_____ ☐ _____
_____ ☐ _____
_____ ☐ _____
_____ ☐ _____

13 TUESDAY

_____ ☐ _____
_____ ☐ _____
_____ ☐ _____
_____ ☐ _____
_____ ☐ _____
_____ ☐ _____
_____ ☐ _____
_____ ☐ _____
_____ ☐ _____
_____ ☐ _____
_____ ☐ _____

14 WEDNESDAY

_____ ☐ _____
_____ ☐ _____
_____ ☐ _____
_____ ☐ _____
_____ ☐ _____
_____ ☐ _____
_____ ☐ _____
_____ ☐ _____
_____ ☐ _____
_____ ☐ _____
_____ ☐ _____

15 THURSDAY

☐
☐
☐
☐
☐
☐
☐
☐
☐
☐
☐

16 FRIDAY

☐
☐
☐
☐
☐
☐
☐
☐
☐
☐
☐

17 SATURDAY

18 SUNDAY

April 2021

19 MONDAY

☐
☐
☐
☐
☐
☐
☐
☐
☐
☐
☐

20 TUESDAY

☐
☐
☐
☐
☐
☐
☐
☐
☐
☐
☐

21 WEDNESDAY

☐
☐
☐
☐
☐
☐
☐
☐
☐
☐
☐

April 2021

22 THURSDAY

Earth Day

- ☐
- ☐
- ☐
- ☐
- ☐
- ☐
- ☐
- ☐
- ☐
- ☐
- ☐

23 FRIDAY

- ☐
- ☐
- ☐
- ☐
- ☐
- ☐
- ☐
- ☐
- ☐
- ☐
- ☐

24 SATURDAY

25 SUNDAY

April 2021

26 MONDAY

☐
☐
☐
☐
☐
☐
☐
☐
☐
☐
☐

27 TUESDAY

☐
☐
☐
☐
☐
☐
☐
☐
☐
☐
☐

28 WEDNESDAY

☐
☐
☐
☐
☐
☐
☐
☐
☐
☐
☐
☐

April 2021

29 THURSDAY

- [ ]
- [ ]
- [ ]
- [ ]
- [ ]
- [ ]
- [ ]
- [ ]
- [ ]
- [ ]
- [ ]

30 FRIDAY

- [ ]
- [ ]
- [ ]
- [ ]
- [ ]
- [ ]
- [ ]
- [ ]
- [ ]
- [ ]
- [ ]

1 SATURDAY

2 SUNDAY

May 2021

SUNDAY	MONDAY	TUESDAY	WEDNESDAY
2	3	4	5
9 Mother's Day	10	11	12
16	17	18	19
23	24	25	26
30	31 Memorial Day		

THURSDAY	FRIDAY	SATURDAY	NOTES
		1	
6	7	8	
13	14	15	
20	21	22	
27	28	29	

May 2021

3 MONDAY

☐
☐
☐
☐
☐
☐
☐
☐
☐
☐
☐

4 TUESDAY

☐
☐
☐
☐
☐
☐
☐
☐
☐
☐
☐

5 WEDNESDAY

☐
☐
☐
☐
☐
☐
☐
☐
☐
☐
☐

May 2021

6 THURSDAY

☐
☐
☐
☐
☐
☐
☐
☐
☐
☐
☐

7 FRIDAY

☐
☐
☐
☐
☐
☐
☐
☐
☐
☐
☐

8 SATURDAY

9 SUNDAY

Mother's Day

May 2021

10 MONDAY

_____
_____
_____
_____
_____
_____
_____
_____
_____
_____

☐
☐
☐
☐
☐
☐
☐
☐
☐
☐
☐

11 TUESDAY

_____
_____
_____
_____
_____
_____
_____
_____
_____
_____

☐
☐
☐
☐
☐
☐
☐
☐
☐
☐
☐

12 WEDNESDAY

_____
_____
_____
_____
_____
_____
_____
_____
_____
_____

☐
☐
☐
☐
☐
☐
☐
☐
☐
☐
☐

May 2021

13 **THURSDAY**

☐
☐
☐
☐
☐
☐
☐
☐
☐
☐
☐

14 **FRIDAY**

☐
☐
☐
☐
☐
☐
☐
☐
☐
☐
☐

15 **SATURDAY**

16 **SUNDAY**

May 2021

17 MONDAY

☐
☐
☐
☐
☐
☐
☐
☐
☐
☐

18 TUESDAY

☐
☐
☐
☐
☐
☐
☐
☐
☐
☐
☐

19 WEDNESDAY

☐
☐
☐
☐
☐
☐
☐
☐
☐
☐
☐

May 2021

20 THURSDAY

- [ ]
- [ ]
- [ ]
- [ ]
- [ ]
- [ ]
- [ ]
- [ ]
- [ ]
- [ ]
- [ ]

21 FRIDAY

- [ ]
- [ ]
- [ ]
- [ ]
- [ ]
- [ ]
- [ ]
- [ ]
- [ ]
- [ ]
- [ ]

22 SATURDAY

23 SUNDAY

May 2021

24 MONDAY

☐
☐
☐
☐
☐
☐
☐
☐
☐
☐
☐

25 TUESDAY

☐
☐
☐
☐
☐
☐
☐
☐
☐
☐
☐

26 WEDNESDAY

☐
☐
☐
☐
☐
☐
☐
☐
☐
☐
☐

May 2021

27 THURSDAY

☐
☐
☐
☐
☐
☐
☐
☐
☐
☐
☐

28 FRIDAY

☐
☐
☐
☐
☐
☐
☐
☐
☐
☐
☐

29 SATURDAY

30 SUNDAY

June 2021

SUNDAY	MONDAY	TUESDAY	WEDNESDAY
		1	2
6	7	8	9
13	14 Flag Day	15	16
20 Father's Day	21 First Day of Summer	22	23
27	28	29	30

THURSDAY	FRIDAY	SATURDAY	NOTES
3	4	5	
10	11	12	
17	18	19	
24	25	26	

May 2021

31 MONDAY

Memorial Day

☐
☐
☐
☐
☐
☐
☐
☐
☐
☐
☐

1 TUESDAY

☐
☐
☐
☐
☐
☐
☐
☐
☐
☐
☐

2 WEDNESDAY

☐
☐
☐
☐
☐
☐
☐
☐
☐
☐
☐

June 2021

3 **THURSDAY**

☐
☐
☐
☐
☐
☐
☐
☐
☐
☐
☐
☐

4 **FRIDAY**

☐
☐
☐
☐
☐
☐
☐
☐
☐
☐
☐

5 **SATURDAY**

6 **SUNDAY**

June 2021

7 **MONDAY**

- [ ]
- [ ]
- [ ]
- [ ]
- [ ]
- [ ]
- [ ]
- [ ]
- [ ]
- [ ]
- [ ]

8 **TUESDAY**

- [ ]
- [ ]
- [ ]
- [ ]
- [ ]
- [ ]
- [ ]
- [ ]
- [ ]
- [ ]
- [ ]

9 **WEDNESDAY**

- [ ]
- [ ]
- [ ]
- [ ]
- [ ]
- [ ]
- [ ]
- [ ]
- [ ]
- [ ]
- [ ]

June 2021

10 THURSDAY

☐
☐
☐
☐
☐
☐
☐
☐
☐
☐
☐

11 FRIDAY

☐
☐
☐
☐
☐
☐
☐
☐
☐
☐
☐

12 SATURDAY

13 SUNDAY

June 2021

14 **MONDAY**

Flag Day

☐
☐
☐
☐
☐
☐
☐
☐
☐
☐
☐

15 **TUESDAY**

☐
☐
☐
☐
☐
☐
☐
☐
☐
☐
☐

16 **WEDNESDAY**

☐
☐
☐
☐
☐
☐
☐
☐
☐
☐
☐

June 2021

17 THURSDAY

☐
☐
☐
☐
☐
☐
☐
☐
☐
☐
☐

18 FRIDAY

☐
☐
☐
☐
☐
☐
☐
☐
☐
☐
☐

19 SATURDAY

20 SUNDAY

Father's Day

June 2021

21 MONDAY

First Day of Summer

☐
☐
☐
☐
☐
☐
☐
☐
☐
☐
☐

22 TUESDAY

☐
☐
☐
☐
☐
☐
☐
☐
☐
☐
☐
☐

23 WEDNESDAY

☐
☐
☐
☐
☐
☐
☐
☐
☐
☐
☐

24 THURSDAY

- [ ]
- [ ]
- [ ]
- [ ]
- [ ]
- [ ]
- [ ]
- [ ]
- [ ]
- [ ]
- [ ]

25 FRIDAY

- [ ]
- [ ]
- [ ]
- [ ]
- [ ]
- [ ]
- [ ]
- [ ]
- [ ]
- [ ]
- [ ]

26 SATURDAY

27 SUNDAY

July 2021

SUNDAY	MONDAY	TUESDAY	WEDNESDAY
4 Independence Day	**5**	**6**	**7**
11	**12**	**13**	**14**
18	**19**	**20**	**21**
25	**26**	**27**	**28**

THURSDAY	FRIDAY	SATURDAY	NOTES
1	2	3	
8	9	10	
15	16	17	
22	23	24	
29	30	31	

June 2021

28 MONDAY

☐
☐
☐
☐
☐
☐
☐
☐
☐
☐
☐

29 TUESDAY

☐
☐
☐
☐
☐
☐
☐
☐
☐
☐
☐

30 WEDNESDAY

☐
☐
☐
☐
☐
☐
☐
☐
☐
☐
☐

July 2021

1 THURSDAY

_____
_____
_____
_____
_____
_____
_____
_____
_____
_____

☐ _____
☐ _____
☐ _____
☐ _____
☐ _____
☐ _____
☐ _____
☐ _____
☐ _____
☐ _____
☐ _____

2 FRIDAY

_____
_____
_____
_____
_____
_____
_____
_____
_____
_____

☐ _____
☐ _____
☐ _____
☐ _____
☐ _____
☐ _____
☐ _____
☐ _____
☐ _____
☐ _____
☐ _____

3 SATURDAY

_____
_____
_____
_____
_____
_____
_____
_____

4 SUNDAY

Independence Day

_____
_____
_____
_____
_____
_____
_____
_____

July 2021

5 **MONDAY**

☐
☐
☐
☐
☐
☐
☐
☐
☐
☐
☐

6 **TUESDAY**

☐
☐
☐
☐
☐
☐
☐
☐
☐
☐
☐

7 **WEDNESDAY**

☐
☐
☐
☐
☐
☐
☐
☐
☐
☐
☐

8 **THURSDAY**

- ☐
- ☐
- ☐
- ☐
- ☐
- ☐
- ☐
- ☐
- ☐
- ☐
- ☐

9 **FRIDAY**

- ☐
- ☐
- ☐
- ☐
- ☐
- ☐
- ☐
- ☐
- ☐
- ☐
- ☐

10 **SATURDAY**

11 **SUNDAY**

July 2021

12 MONDAY

☐
☐
☐
☐
☐
☐
☐
☐
☐
☐
☐

13 TUESDAY

☐
☐
☐
☐
☐
☐
☐
☐
☐
☐
☐

14 WEDNESDAY

☐
☐
☐
☐
☐
☐
☐
☐
☐
☐
☐

15 THURSDAY

- [ ]
- [ ]
- [ ]
- [ ]
- [ ]
- [ ]
- [ ]
- [ ]
- [ ]
- [ ]
- [ ]

16 FRIDAY

- [ ]
- [ ]
- [ ]
- [ ]
- [ ]
- [ ]
- [ ]
- [ ]
- [ ]
- [ ]
- [ ]

17 SATURDAY

18 SUNDAY

July 2021

19 MONDAY

☐
☐
☐
☐
☐
☐
☐
☐
☐
☐
☐

20 TUESDAY

☐
☐
☐
☐
☐
☐
☐
☐
☐
☐
☐

21 WEDNESDAY

☐
☐
☐
☐
☐
☐
☐
☐
☐
☐
☐

22 THURSDAY

- [ ]
- [ ]
- [ ]
- [ ]
- [ ]
- [ ]
- [ ]
- [ ]
- [ ]
- [ ]
- [ ]

23 FRIDAY

- [ ]
- [ ]
- [ ]
- [ ]
- [ ]
- [ ]
- [ ]
- [ ]
- [ ]
- [ ]
- [ ]

24 SATURDAY

25 SUNDAY

July 2021

26 **MONDAY**

☐
☐
☐
☐
☐
☐
☐
☐
☐
☐
☐

27 **TUESDAY**

☐
☐
☐
☐
☐
☐
☐
☐
☐
☐
☐

28 **WEDNESDAY**

☐
☐
☐
☐
☐
☐
☐
☐
☐
☐
☐

29 THURSDAY

☐
☐
☐
☐
☐
☐
☐
☐
☐
☐
☐

30 FRIDAY

☐
☐
☐
☐
☐
☐
☐
☐
☐
☐
☐

31 SATURDAY

1 SUNDAY

August 2021

SUNDAY	MONDAY	TUESDAY	WEDNESDAY
1	2	3	4
8	9	10	11
15	16	17	18
22	23	24	25
29	30	31	

THURSDAY	FRIDAY	SATURDAY	NOTES
5	6	7	
12	13	14	
19	20	21	
26	27	28	

August 2021

2 MONDAY

☐
☐
☐
☐
☐
☐
☐
☐
☐
☐
☐

3 TUESDAY

☐
☐
☐
☐
☐
☐
☐
☐
☐
☐
☐

4 WEDNESDAY

☐
☐
☐
☐
☐
☐
☐
☐
☐
☐
☐

5 THURSDAY

☐
☐
☐
☐
☐
☐
☐
☐
☐
☐
☐

6 FRIDAY

☐
☐
☐
☐
☐
☐
☐
☐
☐
☐
☐

7 SATURDAY

8 SUNDAY

August 2021

9 MONDAY

☐
☐
☐
☐
☐
☐
☐
☐
☐
☐
☐

10 TUESDAY

☐
☐
☐
☐
☐
☐
☐
☐
☐
☐
☐

11 WEDNESDAY

☐
☐
☐
☐
☐
☐
☐
☐
☐
☐
☐

12 **THURSDAY**

☐
☐
☐
☐
☐
☐
☐
☐
☐
☐
☐

13 **FRIDAY**

☐
☐
☐
☐
☐
☐
☐
☐
☐
☐
☐

14 **SATURDAY**

15 **SUNDAY**

August 2021

16 MONDAY

_____ ☐
_____ ☐
_____ ☐
_____ ☐
_____ ☐
_____ ☐
_____ ☐
_____ ☐
_____ ☐
_____ ☐
_____ ☐

17 TUESDAY

_____ ☐
_____ ☐
_____ ☐
_____ ☐
_____ ☐
_____ ☐
_____ ☐
_____ ☐
_____ ☐
_____ ☐
_____ ☐

18 WEDNESDAY

_____ ☐
_____ ☐
_____ ☐
_____ ☐
_____ ☐
_____ ☐
_____ ☐
_____ ☐
_____ ☐
_____ ☐
_____ ☐

August 2021

19 THURSDAY

- [ ]
- [ ]
- [ ]
- [ ]
- [ ]
- [ ]
- [ ]
- [ ]
- [ ]
- [ ]
- [ ]

20 FRIDAY

- [ ]
- [ ]
- [ ]
- [ ]
- [ ]
- [ ]
- [ ]
- [ ]
- [ ]
- [ ]
- [ ]

21 SATURDAY

22 SUNDAY

August 2021

23 **MONDAY**

☐
☐
☐
☐
☐
☐
☐
☐
☐
☐
☐

24 **TUESDAY**

☐
☐
☐
☐
☐
☐
☐
☐
☐
☐
☐

25 **WEDNESDAY**

☐
☐
☐
☐
☐
☐
☐
☐
☐
☐
☐

August 2021

26 THURSDAY

☐
☐
☐
☐
☐
☐
☐
☐
☐
☐
☐

27 FRIDAY

☐
☐
☐
☐
☐
☐
☐
☐
☐
☐
☐

28 SATURDAY

29 SUNDAY

September 2021

SUNDAY	MONDAY	TUESDAY	WEDNESDAY
			1
5	**6** Labor Day Rosh Hashanah, Begins at Sunset	**7**	**8**
12 Grandparents Day	**13**	**14**	**15** Yom Kippur, Begins at Sunset
19	**20**	**21**	**22** First Day of Autumn
26	**27**	**28**	**29**

THURSDAY	FRIDAY	SATURDAY	NOTES
2	**3**	**4**	
9	**10**	**11** Patriot Day	
16	**17**	**18**	
23	**24**	**25**	
30			

August 2021

30 MONDAY

☐
☐
☐
☐
☐
☐
☐
☐
☐
☐
☐

31 TUESDAY

☐
☐
☐
☐
☐
☐
☐
☐
☐
☐
☐

1 WEDNESDAY

☐
☐
☐
☐
☐
☐
☐
☐
☐
☐
☐

September 2021

2 THURSDAY

☐
☐
☐
☐
☐
☐
☐
☐
☐
☐
☐

3 FRIDAY

☐
☐
☐
☐
☐
☐
☐
☐
☐
☐
☐
☐

4 SATURDAY

5 SUNDAY

September 2021

6 **MONDAY**

Labor Day

Rosh Hashanah, Begins at Sunset

☐
☐
☐
☐
☐
☐
☐
☐
☐
☐
☐

7 **TUESDAY**

☐
☐
☐
☐
☐
☐
☐
☐
☐
☐
☐

8 **WEDNESDAY**

☐
☐
☐
☐
☐
☐
☐
☐
☐
☐
☐

September 2021

9 THURSDAY

☐
☐
☐
☐
☐
☐
☐
☐
☐
☐
☐

10 FRIDAY

☐
☐
☐
☐
☐
☐
☐
☐
☐
☐
☐

11 SATURDAY

Patriot Day

12 SUNDAY

Grandparents Day

September 2021

13 **MONDAY**

- [ ]
- [ ]
- [ ]
- [ ]
- [ ]
- [ ]
- [ ]
- [ ]
- [ ]
- [ ]
- [ ]

14 **TUESDAY**

- [ ]
- [ ]
- [ ]
- [ ]
- [ ]
- [ ]
- [ ]
- [ ]
- [ ]
- [ ]
- [ ]

15 **WEDNESDAY**

Yom Kippur, Begins at Sunset

- [ ]
- [ ]
- [ ]
- [ ]
- [ ]
- [ ]
- [ ]
- [ ]
- [ ]
- [ ]
- [ ]

September 2021

16 THURSDAY

_____
_____
_____
_____
_____
_____
_____
_____
_____
_____
_____

☐
☐
☐
☐
☐
☐
☐
☐
☐
☐
☐

17 FRIDAY

_____
_____
_____
_____
_____
_____
_____
_____
_____
_____
_____
_____

☐
☐
☐
☐
☐
☐
☐
☐
☐
☐
☐

18 SATURDAY

_____
_____
_____
_____
_____
_____
_____
_____
_____

19 SUNDAY

_____
_____
_____
_____
_____
_____
_____
_____

September 2021

20 MONDAY

- [ ]
- [ ]
- [ ]
- [ ]
- [ ]
- [ ]
- [ ]
- [ ]
- [ ]
- [ ]
- [ ]

21 TUESDAY

- [ ]
- [ ]
- [ ]
- [ ]
- [ ]
- [ ]
- [ ]
- [ ]
- [ ]
- [ ]
- [ ]

22 WEDNESDAY

First Day of Autumn

- [ ]
- [ ]
- [ ]
- [ ]
- [ ]
- [ ]
- [ ]
- [ ]
- [ ]
- [ ]
- [ ]

September 2021

23 THURSDAY

- [ ]
- [ ]
- [ ]
- [ ]
- [ ]
- [ ]
- [ ]
- [ ]
- [ ]
- [ ]
- [ ]

24 FRIDAY

- [ ]
- [ ]
- [ ]
- [ ]
- [ ]
- [ ]
- [ ]
- [ ]
- [ ]
- [ ]
- [ ]

25 SATURDAY

26 SUNDAY

September 2021

27 MONDAY

☐
☐
☐
☐
☐
☐
☐
☐
☐
☐

28 TUESDAY

☐
☐
☐
☐
☐
☐
☐
☐
☐
☐
☐

29 WEDNESDAY

☐
☐
☐
☐
☐
☐
☐
☐
☐
☐
☐

September 2021

30 THURSDAY

☐
☐
☐
☐
☐
☐
☐
☐
☐
☐
☐

1 FRIDAY

☐
☐
☐
☐
☐
☐
☐
☐
☐
☐
☐

2 SATURDAY

3 SUNDAY

October 2021

SUNDAY	MONDAY	TUESDAY	WEDNESDAY
3	4	5	6
10	11 Columbus Day	12	13
17	18	19	20
24	25	26	27
31 Halloween			

THURSDAY	FRIDAY	SATURDAY	NOTES
	1	2	
7	8	9	
14	15	16	
21	22	23	
28	29	30	

October 2021

4 **MONDAY**

☐
☐
☐
☐
☐
☐
☐
☐
☐
☐
☐

5 **TUESDAY**

☐
☐
☐
☐
☐
☐
☐
☐
☐
☐
☐

6 **WEDNESDAY**

☐
☐
☐
☐
☐
☐
☐
☐
☐
☐
☐

7 **THURSDAY**

☐
☐
☐
☐
☐
☐
☐
☐
☐
☐
☐

8 **FRIDAY**

☐
☐
☐
☐
☐
☐
☐
☐
☐
☐
☐

9 **SATURDAY**

10 **SUNDAY**

October 2021

11 MONDAY

Columbus Day

☐
☐
☐
☐
☐
☐
☐
☐
☐
☐
☐

12 TUESDAY

☐
☐
☐
☐
☐
☐
☐
☐
☐
☐
☐
☐

13 WEDNESDAY

☐
☐
☐
☐
☐
☐
☐
☐
☐
☐
☐

14 THURSDAY

_____

☐
☐
☐
☐
☐
☐
☐
☐
☐
☐
☐

15 FRIDAY

_____

☐
☐
☐
☐
☐
☐
☐
☐
☐
☐
☐

16 SATURDAY

17 SUNDAY

October 2021

18 MONDAY

☐
☐
☐
☐
☐
☐
☐
☐
☐
☐
☐

19 TUESDAY

☐
☐
☐
☐
☐
☐
☐
☐
☐
☐
☐

20 WEDNESDAY

☐
☐
☐
☐
☐
☐
☐
☐
☐
☐
☐

October 2021

21 THURSDAY

☐
☐
☐
☐
☐
☐
☐
☐
☐
☐
☐

22 FRIDAY

☐
☐
☐
☐
☐
☐
☐
☐
☐
☐
☐

23 SATURDAY

24 SUNDAY

October 2021

25 MONDAY

☐
☐
☐
☐
☐
☐
☐
☐
☐
☐
☐

26 TUESDAY

☐
☐
☐
☐
☐
☐
☐
☐
☐
☐
☐

27 WEDNESDAY

☐
☐
☐
☐
☐
☐
☐
☐
☐
☐
☐

October 2021

28 THURSDAY

- [ ]
- [ ]
- [ ]
- [ ]
- [ ]
- [ ]
- [ ]
- [ ]
- [ ]
- [ ]
- [ ]

29 FRIDAY

- [ ]
- [ ]
- [ ]
- [ ]
- [ ]
- [ ]
- [ ]
- [ ]
- [ ]
- [ ]
- [ ]

30 SATURDAY

31 SUNDAY

Halloween

November 2021

SUNDAY	MONDAY	TUESDAY	WEDNESDAY
	1	**2** Election Day	**3**
7 Daylight Saving Time Ends	**8**	**9**	**10**
14	**15**	**16**	**17**
21	**22**	**23**	**24**
28 Hanukkah, Begins at Sunset	**29**	**30**	

THURSDAY	FRIDAY	SATURDAY	NOTES
4	**5**	**6**	
11 Veterans Day	**12**	**13**	
18	**19**	**20**	
25 Thanksgiving Day	**26**	**27**	

November 2021

1 MONDAY

☐
☐
☐
☐
☐
☐
☐
☐
☐
☐
☐

2 TUESDAY

Election Day

☐
☐
☐
☐
☐
☐
☐
☐
☐
☐
☐

3 WEDNESDAY

☐
☐
☐
☐
☐
☐
☐
☐
☐
☐
☐

November 2021

4 THURSDAY

- [ ]
- [ ]
- [ ]
- [ ]
- [ ]
- [ ]
- [ ]
- [ ]
- [ ]
- [ ]
- [ ]

5 FRIDAY

- [ ]
- [ ]
- [ ]
- [ ]
- [ ]
- [ ]
- [ ]
- [ ]
- [ ]
- [ ]
- [ ]

6 SATURDAY

7 SUNDAY

Daylight Saving Time Ends

November 2021

8 **MONDAY**

☐
☐
☐
☐
☐
☐
☐
☐
☐
☐
☐

9 **TUESDAY**

☐
☐
☐
☐
☐
☐
☐
☐
☐
☐
☐

10 **WEDNESDAY**

☐
☐
☐
☐
☐
☐
☐
☐
☐
☐
☐

November 2021

11 THURSDAY

Veterans Day

- [ ]
- [ ]
- [ ]
- [ ]
- [ ]
- [ ]
- [ ]
- [ ]
- [ ]
- [ ]
- [ ]

12 FRIDAY

- [ ]
- [ ]
- [ ]
- [ ]
- [ ]
- [ ]
- [ ]
- [ ]
- [ ]
- [ ]
- [ ]

13 SATURDAY

14 SUNDAY

November 2021

15 MONDAY

☐
☐
☐
☐
☐
☐
☐
☐
☐
☐
☐

16 TUESDAY

☐
☐
☐
☐
☐
☐
☐
☐
☐
☐
☐

17 WEDNESDAY

☐
☐
☐
☐
☐
☐
☐
☐
☐
☐
☐

18 THURSDAY

☐
☐
☐
☐
☐
☐
☐
☐
☐
☐
☐

19 FRIDAY

☐
☐
☐
☐
☐
☐
☐
☐
☐
☐
☐

20 SATURDAY

21 SUNDAY

November 2021

22 MONDAY

☐
☐
☐
☐
☐
☐
☐
☐
☐
☐
☐

23 TUESDAY

☐
☐
☐
☐
☐
☐
☐
☐
☐
☐
☐

24 WEDNESDAY

☐
☐
☐
☐
☐
☐
☐
☐
☐
☐
☐

November 2021

25 THURSDAY
Thanksgiving Day

- [ ]
- [ ]
- [ ]
- [ ]
- [ ]
- [ ]
- [ ]
- [ ]
- [ ]
- [ ]
- [ ]

26 FRIDAY

- [ ]
- [ ]
- [ ]
- [ ]
- [ ]
- [ ]
- [ ]
- [ ]
- [ ]
- [ ]
- [ ]

27 SATURDAY

28 SUNDAY
Hanukkah, Begins at Sunset

December 2021

SUNDAY	MONDAY	TUESDAY	WEDNESDAY
			1
5	6	7	8
12	13	14	15
19	20	21 First Day of Winter	22
26 Kwanzaa Begins	27	28	29

THURSDAY	FRIDAY	SATURDAY	NOTES
2	**3**	**4**	
9	**10**	**11**	
16	**17**	**18**	
23	**24**	**25** Christmas Day	
30	**31** New Year's Eve		

November 2021

29 MONDAY

☐
☐
☐
☐
☐
☐
☐
☐
☐
☐
☐

30 TUESDAY

☐
☐
☐
☐
☐
☐
☐
☐
☐
☐
☐

1 WEDNESDAY

☐
☐
☐
☐
☐
☐
☐
☐
☐
☐
☐

December 2021

2 THURSDAY

- [ ]
- [ ]
- [ ]
- [ ]
- [ ]
- [ ]
- [ ]
- [ ]
- [ ]
- [ ]
- [ ]

3 FRIDAY

- [ ]
- [ ]
- [ ]
- [ ]
- [ ]
- [ ]
- [ ]
- [ ]
- [ ]
- [ ]
- [ ]

4 SATURDAY

5 SUNDAY

December 2021

6 **MONDAY**

☐
☐
☐
☐
☐
☐
☐
☐
☐
☐
☐

7 **TUESDAY**

☐
☐
☐
☐
☐
☐
☐
☐
☐
☐
☐

8 **WEDNESDAY**

☐
☐
☐
☐
☐
☐
☐
☐
☐
☐
☐

December 2021

9 THURSDAY

_____
_____
_____
_____
_____
_____
_____
_____
_____
_____

☐ _____
☐ _____
☐ _____
☐ _____
☐ _____
☐ _____
☐ _____
☐ _____
☐ _____
☐ _____
☐ _____

10 FRIDAY

_____
_____
_____
_____
_____
_____
_____
_____
_____
_____
_____

☐ _____
☐ _____
☐ _____
☐ _____
☐ _____
☐ _____
☐ _____
☐ _____
☐ _____
☐ _____
☐ _____

11 SATURDAY

_____
_____
_____
_____
_____
_____
_____
_____
_____
_____

12 SUNDAY

_____
_____
_____
_____
_____
_____
_____
_____
_____
_____

December 2021

13 MONDAY

☐
☐
☐
☐
☐
☐
☐
☐
☐
☐
☐

14 TUESDAY

☐
☐
☐
☐
☐
☐
☐
☐
☐
☐
☐

15 WEDNESDAY

☐
☐
☐
☐
☐
☐
☐
☐
☐
☐
☐

December 2021

16 THURSDAY

☐
☐
☐
☐
☐
☐
☐
☐
☐
☐
☐

17 FRIDAY

☐
☐
☐
☐
☐
☐
☐
☐
☐
☐
☐

18 SATURDAY

19 SUNDAY

December 2021

20 MONDAY

_____
_____
_____
_____
_____
_____
_____
_____
_____
_____
_____

☐
☐
☐
☐
☐
☐
☐
☐
☐
☐
☐

21 TUESDAY

First Day of Winter

_____
_____
_____
_____
_____
_____
_____
_____
_____
_____
_____

☐
☐
☐
☐
☐
☐
☐
☐
☐
☐
☐

22 WEDNESDAY

_____
_____
_____
_____
_____
_____
_____
_____
_____
_____
_____

☐
☐
☐
☐
☐
☐
☐
☐
☐
☐
☐

December 2021

23 THURSDAY

☐
☐
☐
☐
☐
☐
☐
☐
☐
☐
☐

24 FRIDAY

☐
☐
☐
☐
☐
☐
☐
☐
☐
☐
☐

25 SATURDAY

Christmas Day

26 SUNDAY

Kwanzaa Begins

December 2021

27 MONDAY

☐
☐
☐
☐
☐
☐
☐
☐
☐
☐
☐

28 TUESDAY

☐
☐
☐
☐
☐
☐
☐
☐
☐
☐
☐

29 WEDNESDAY

☐
☐
☐
☐
☐
☐
☐
☐
☐
☐
☐

December 2021

30 THURSDAY

- [ ]
- [ ]
- [ ]
- [ ]
- [ ]
- [ ]
- [ ]
- [ ]
- [ ]
- [ ]
- [ ]

31 FRIDAY

New Year's Eve

- [ ]
- [ ]
- [ ]
- [ ]
- [ ]
- [ ]
- [ ]
- [ ]
- [ ]
- [ ]
- [ ]

1 SATURDAY

New Year's Day

2 SUNDAY

NOTES

2022

JANUARY

SUN	MON	TUE	WED	THU	FRI	SAT
						1
2	3	4	5	6	7	8
9	10	11	12	13	14	15
16	17	18	19	20	21	22
23	24	25	26	27	28	29
30	31					

FEBRUARY

SUN	MON	TUE	WED	THU	FRI	SAT
		1	2	3	4	5
6	7	8	9	10	11	12
13	14	15	16	17	18	19
20	21	22	23	24	25	26
27	28					

MARCH

SUN	MON	TUE	WED	THU	FRI	SAT
		1	2	3	4	5
6	7	8	9	10	11	12
13	14	15	16	17	18	19
20	21	22	23	24	25	26
27	28	29	30	31		

APRIL

SUN	MON	TUE	WED	THU	FRI	SAT
					1	2
3	4	5	6	7	8	9
10	11	12	13	14	15	16
17	18	19	20	21	22	23
24	25	26	27	28	29	30

MAY

SUN	MON	TUE	WED	THU	FRI	SAT
1	2	3	4	5	6	7
8	9	10	11	12	13	14
15	16	17	18	19	20	21
22	23	24	25	26	27	28
29	30	31				

JUNE

SUN	MON	TUE	WED	THU	FRI	SAT
			1	2	3	4
5	6	7	8	9	10	11
12	13	14	15	16	17	18
19	20	21	22	23	24	25
26	27	28	29	30		

JULY

SUN	MON	TUE	WED	THU	FRI	SAT
					1	2
3	4	5	6	7	8	9
10	11	12	13	14	15	16
17	18	19	20	21	22	23
24	25	26	27	28	29	30
31						

AUGUST

SUN	MON	TUE	WED	THU	FRI	SAT
	1	2	3	4	5	6
7	8	9	10	11	12	13
14	15	16	17	18	19	20
21	22	23	24	25	26	27
28	29	30	31			

SEPTEMBER

SUN	MON	TUE	WED	THU	FRI	SAT
				1	2	3
4	5	6	7	8	9	10
11	12	13	14	15	16	17
18	19	20	21	22	23	24
25	26	27	28	29	30	

OCTOBER

SUN	MON	TUE	WED	THU	FRI	SAT
						1
2	3	4	5	6	7	8
9	10	11	12	13	14	15
16	17	18	19	20	21	22
23	24	25	26	27	28	29
30	31					

NOVEMBER

SUN	MON	TUE	WED	THU	FRI	SAT
		1	2	3	4	5
6	7	8	9	10	11	12
13	14	15	16	17	18	19
20	21	22	23	24	25	26
27	28	29	30			

DECEMBER

SUN	MON	TUE	WED	THU	FRI	SAT
				1	2	3
4	5	6	7	8	9	10
11	12	13	14	15	16	17
18	19	20	21	22	23	24
25	26	27	28	29	30	31

CPSIA information can be obtained
at www.ICGtesting.com
Printed in the USA
BVHW010824051020
590084BV00016B/341